motivation

Poetry & Patchwork

reflection

inspiration

connection

Gyleen X. Fitzgerald & James W. Pryde, Jr.

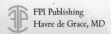
FPI Publishing
Havre de Grace, MD

Poetry and Patchwork: Motivation, Inspiration, Connection, Reflection
by Gyleen X. Fitzgerald and James W. Pryde, Jr.

Published by FPI Publishing
PO Box 247, Havre de Grace, MD 21078
www.ColourfulStitches.com

Cover and interior design by Pneuma Books, LLC
Visit www.pneumabooks.com for more information.

Publisher's Cataloging-in-Publication Data
(Prepared by The Donohue Group, Inc.)

Fitzgerald, Gyleen X.
　　Poetry & patchwork : motivation, inspiration, connection, reflection
/ Gyleen X. Fitzgerald & James W. Pryde, Jr.

　　　p. : ill. ;　cm.
　　ISBN-13: 978-0-9768215-2-6
　　ISBN-10: 0-9768215-2-4

1. Haiku, American—21st century. 2. Quilts—Pictorial works. I.
Pryde, James W., Jr. II. Title. III. Title: Poetry and patchwork.

PS3556.I83 P64 2005
811.6
　　　　　　　　　　　　　　　　　LCCN: 2005931571

10　09　08　07　06　05　　　　　　6　5　4　3　2　1

credits

Hand Me Downs
Designed and pieced by Joan Baummer, Churchville, MD

Turtle Diamond
From the collection of Denise and Cleosie Kirkland, Voorhees, NJ

Olé
Machine pieced by Joan Baummer, Churchville, MD

Carpenter's Square
From the collection of Holy Trinity Episcopal Church, Churchville, MD
Designed by Peg Bingham, Akron, OH

Happy 69th Birthday
From the collection of Fonzora S. Fitzgerald, Havre de Grace, MD

Garden in the Mist
Professionally machine quilted by Peg Dougherty, Pylesville, MD

Without Thorns
Original design by Fran Kordek, Elkins, WV

❧

Capture just one thought
In seventeen syllables.
Your turn to ponder.

— • —

Take the 1st Step
Coyleen ☺ 04/06

dedication

∞

To our parents for
creating potential and
expecting results.

— • —

preface

—•—

In the winter of 2004, I issued a challenge. I told James that I could write more haiku — more quickly — than he could — and he's a writer. Moreover, James is an introspective writer — and reader — who likes to keep things simple. He'll never wear more than two colors at the same time, his office is sparse, and he loves to write haiku.

I, on the other hand, am a quilter and a dreamer. I am also an engineer, which means I love to solve

vii

problems and control chaos. Whether it's developing repeatable steps to construct something or transforming a broken teapot into garden art or using hundreds of fabrics in one patchwork quilt, rhythm and purpose are my tools.

I use those same tools for haiku writing. Haiku appear to be simple, but they pack a punch. They are notable for being compressed and suggestive. Haiku record a moment, sensation, or impression in time, and they're often personal.

viii

Because haiku contain repeatable steps, a form
of rhythm, I was certain I could win. James *knew* he
would win because he didn't think a quilter like me
could thrive under the "rules" of haiku. He knew I
like to use hundreds of fabrics in one patchwork
quilt; how would I ever limit myself to a mere
seventeen syllables?

So the challenge was on and the rules were
these: for the haiku, the first two lines must relate
and the third line must relate in a visceral form.

Poetry & Patchwork

The three unrhymed lines of five, seven, and five syllables are to be spoken in a single breath. We each had to write fifty poems; the first one finished would be the winner. We had one year from the start of the challenge to complete all fifty, and the haiku had to be inspired by moments within that year.

The haiku in this collection are our best from that challenge. They represent one thought, one breath, and one vision. We've collected them here with some of my favorite quilts. Quilting and haiku –

x

two forms of art that entangle our minds with infinite possibilities. We hope you enjoy them both.

— • —

inspiration

—•—

Having vision brings forth new and exciting possibilities. Creativity and innovation drive us to believe that all things can be accomplished through diligence and patience. Your great talent lies dormant in the layers of life until you release your inner self and begin to see the cleared path ahead.

By taking the initial steps, your vision gains clarity and momentum drives new insights until potential becomes a reality. Be inspired to forward thinking and stitch a new fabric in your life.

Double X, 2004, w25" x h25"

The Seer

3

Complex by design
Human shadows create art
Enlightened vision.

—·—

Hand Me Downs, 2000, w27" x h24"

Earthly Soul

∽

Shorter days ahead
The fall sun makes long shadows
Clear beauty stills me.

— • —

Turtle Diamond, 2002, w19" x h15"

Forward Momentum

∽

The way is so clear
Although it is not easy
My first step is long.

—•—

1

Olé, 2002, w23" x h23"

Release

∞

Freeing myself now
Living gives me all I need
Structure flies away.

—•—

inspiration

Infinity, 2003, w22" x h22"

Potential

3

Laugh in morning wind
Sip tea in afternoon rain
Dream of tomorrow.

—•—

"

Carpenter's Square, 1998, w30" x h30"

Decisiveness

∽

It is all there now
Stop searching for it so far
All you need you have.

— • —

Africa: Nation of One, 2001, w24" x h27"

Visual Clarity

∽

Tree-painted landscape
Color blended by nature.
Takes my breath away.

—•—

15

Spring, 2002, w28" x h28"

New Beginning

∽

Waiting patiently
In the warming winter day,
Cherry blossoms swell.

— • —

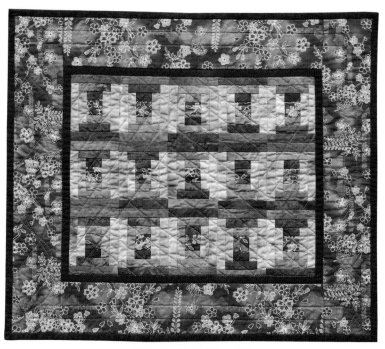

Wisteria, 2000, w21" x h18"

Insight

∽

Momentarily,
Wisdom of ages appears
I am still baffled.

—•—

motivation

— • —

Dreaming with purpose creates the future of possibilities. Your destiny is clearly ahead — awaiting your arrival. Faith and focus coupled with energy will propel you toward your goals. It's the inner strength pushing toward excellence that forges the path to an authentic self.

Release your limits and fully expand your expectations. Greatness is a part of your future. Be strong. Get moving. All you have is all you need. Use it all. Cut your first patch and stitch together your future.

Atlantis, 2005, w35" x h38"

Creativity

∽

Why not always dream
As easy as water boils?
Let our spirits soar.

—•—

Dragonfly, 2002, w16" x h16"

Inner Strength

ॐ

Seeing your bright smile
Encourages growth within
My heart beats stronger.

— • —

Bamboo, 2002, w20" x h20"

Success

∽

Destiny appears
Inspired forward thinking
Replenish my soul.

—•—

Baskets I, 2000, w25" x h25"

Excellence

∽

Limits do abound
The ones for you are out there
Have you met them yet?

—•—

Wheels, 2001, w17" x h17"

Courage

ͼͽ

Under Mother's wing,
Temptation seeks adventure.
Self-confidence born.

—•—

Happy 69ᵗʰ Birthday, 2001, w24" x h27"

Poignant Progress

∞

Smooth cool river rock

Resists temptation to move

Time polished beauty.

— • —

Nine of Hearts, 1997, w21" x h21"

Diversity

∽

Tolerance practice,
Compassion demands a price.
Burden of freedom.

—•—

35

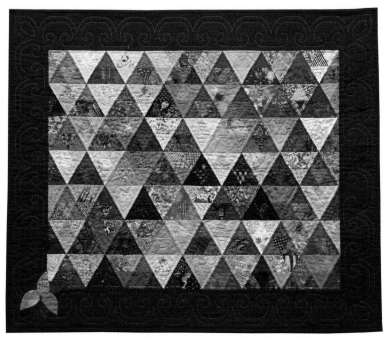

Trillium Charm, 2001, w38" x h32"

Natural Growth

∽

Constantly serving
We grow exponentially
Opportunities abound.

—•—

Rainforest, 2005, w25" x h25"

Liberty

∞

Within the darkness
Eyes shining through the small crack
See the hope in stars.

—•—

con

connection

—•—

Searching near and far for excitement, we unwittingly ignore the blades of grass under our feet and the tree that has grown thirty feet in the ten years that have passed. Make the most of opportunities to enhance relationships with family, friends, neighbors, coworkers, and nature.

Take the present moment and embrace the greatness of each breath. Commune with those who have touched your life and those you can touch. Choose to influence the rhythm of the world. Love the patchwork you create and stitch strong bonds that hold it all together.

Garden in the Mist, 2004, w49" x h49"

Clarity

∽

Symphony of color
The garden beyond the mist
Beauty suspended.

— • —

43

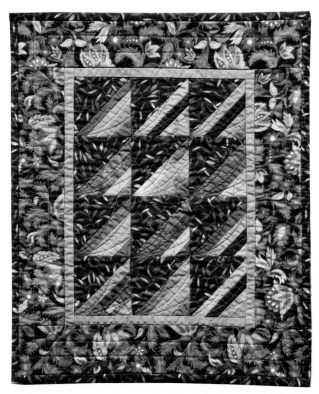

October, 2000, w16" x h18"

Complexity

∽

Joy inside my tears
Seeing the sameness about
It's good to be home.

—•—

ys

Fruits of Handmade Pleasures, 1999, w23" x h23"

Being Yourself

ꝏ

Summer's heat in June
Fruit ripens to perfection
Juice runs down my chin.

— • —

47

connection

Calypso, 2005, w35" x h36"

Happiness

∽

A day's worth of life
Captured by orange lilies
Fills my cup with smiles.

—•—

49

Genesis, 1999, w21" x h21"

Loving Spirit

∽

In my lover's arms
A spider's web grows stronger
My world is complete.

—•—

Without Thorns, 2002, w25" x h25"

Effective Motion

∽

Step into the light
Humming bird beats his wings
God's perfect rhythm.

— • —

Confetti, 2004, w57" x h57"

Cocoon

လ

Silence under white
The storm blows before the calm
Spring quietly hides.

—•—

One Degree of Separation, 2003, w22" x h22"

Unity

∽

Pieces of our life
Embraced, laced, and bound.
We have become one.

— • —

connection

French Provence, 2002, w24" x h27"

Homecoming

ఴ

Wonderful return
Splendid beyond all belief
This is who we are.

— • —

59

reflection

— • —

We spend time accumulating things, friendships, and memories. We search and strive for our own ultimate reality. If we have gained wisdom and become content, is it enough? Are you satisfied with what can be accomplished in a lifetime?

All of your choices have led to this point. Your quilt is complete, or is it? Add more, but you can't take away. When you enthusiastically embrace where you are, the journey can inspire you all over again and another patch is cut.

reflection

Serenity I, 1996, w46" x h46"

Moments

∽

Zen time passes in
A sliver of a second.
Cherished forever.

—•—

reflection

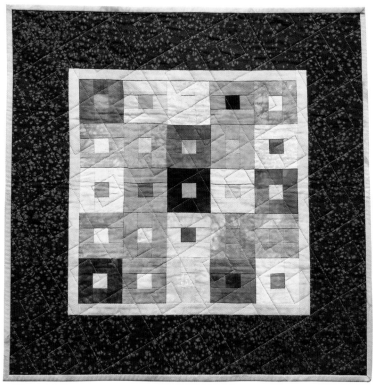

Parallel Universe, 2002, w25" x h25"

Inner Peace

cos

Finished I look in
I am satisfied with me
No more looking out.

—•—

Pandora's Box, 2004, w30" x h34"

Reaching Higher Ground

∽

Looking from up here
Life seems so free and distant
Slowly I come home.

— · —

Shoofly By, 2002, w17" x h23"

Concentration

∽

The sound of water
Echoes loud in each droplet.
I hear the whisper.

—•—

reflection

From Dawn to Dusk, 2002, w25" x h25"

Hope

∽

Dusk dawn daylight signs
Season after season comes
Miraculously.

— • —

Charmed Tumbler, 2001, w14" x h17"

Confusion

∽

Deafening chaos
Paralyzes sound wisdom.
Too tired to think.

—•—

reflection

Vintage Baskets, 2000, w17" x h22"

Life

೭

Living in the past
A shadow of who I was
One spirit flows free.

— • —

15

reflection

Twin Towers, 2001, w19" x h19"

Energy

∞

Between the rain drops
The speed of life moves faster
I am exhausted.

—•—

reflection

Remember Summer, 2002, w17" x h17"

The Future

∽

Look toward the sun
Shadows will fall behind you
Move passed destiny.

— • —

79

About the Authors

Gyleen X. Fitzgerald has been quilting since 1981. She is the recipient of numerous awards, and her quilts have been published in *Patchwork Quilting*, *Quick Quilts*, and *Quilt Almanac*. Through her business, Colourful Stitches, Gyleen offers workshops and lectures and sells notecards as well as hand-dyed fabrics and silk scarves. She says her Quilt of Life — living in Maryland with her husband James and their Boxers — is complete.

James W. Pryde, Jr., is a corporate senior vice president as well as a miler and marathon runner and a writer. His motto reflects his diverse professional and personal interests: "What can't be written can be calculated." James is committed to lifelong learning and passionate about living with the whole body through wellness and spirituality.

The Dream: A Magical Journey in Colourful Stitches
Price: **$**29.95 • ISBN: 0-9768215-1-6

Ordering Information

FPI Publishing books are available online or at your favorite bookstore. Quantity discounts are available to qualifying institutions. All FPI Publishing books are available to the booktrade and educators through all major wholesalers. For more information, visit the website.

Lectures

Discover the art of colour blending, why some bed quilts work and others don't, or customize your own lecture! Visit the website for lecture dates.

Workshops

Gyleen Fitzgerald teaches workshops on colour and value in quilting. For workshop dates and to purchase a pattern, visit the website. Discounts available to quilt shops.

Hand Dyeing

Colourful Stitches produces irresistible colour combinations. Our hand-dyeing process produces distinct, saturated colours, which are unobtainable in the commercial dyeing process. The end result is a 100% colour fast, washable, silky, drapeable scarf, pillow, or expressive cotton in colours to dye for!

www.ColourfulStitches.com

Colour Your World.

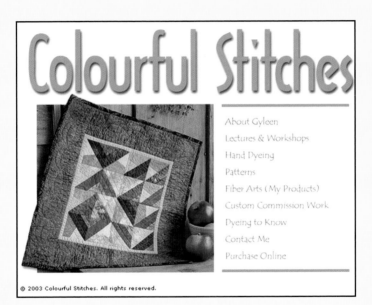

Gyleen is absolutely passionate about quilting!
Visit her on the web for patterns, notecards, signature quilts, silk scarves,
pillows, dinner napkins, socks, workshops, lectures, and much more.

www.ColourfulStitches.com